Jennifer Lopez Biography

The Unstoppable Rise from the Bronx to Global Stardom

David Williams

Table of Contents

Introduction

An Insight into the Life of Jennifer Lopez

Jennifer Lopez, known affectionately as J.Lo, is a name synonymous with glamour, talent, and resilience. Born on July 24, 1969, in the Bronx, New York City, Jennifer Lynn Lopez has transcended her humble beginnings to become a global icon in entertainment and business. Raised in a close-knit Puerto Rican family, Lopez was the middle of three daughters born to Guadalupe Rodríguez and David Lopez. Her parents instilled in her the values of hard work and perseverance, which would later become the cornerstones of her illustrious career.

From a young age, Lopez showed an affinity for performing. She began taking singing and dancing lessons at the age of five, honing her skills in ballet, jazz, and flamenco. Her parents encouraged her passion for the arts while emphasizing the importance of education. Despite the financial constraints of growing up in a working-class neighborhood, Lopez's family prioritized her artistic education, recognizing her potential for greatness.

Lopez's journey to stardom began as a dancer. In her teenage years, she competed in various dance competitions and performed in school musicals. After a brief stint at Baruch College, she decided to pursue her dream full-time, which led to her first major break as a dancer on the television show "In Living Color." As a Fly Girl, Lopez's charisma and talent captured the attention of audiences and industry insiders alike, setting the stage for her future successes.

Transitioning from dance to acting, Lopez's determination and versatility became evident. Her breakthrough role came in 1997, when she portrayed Tejano singer Selena Quintanilla-Pérez in the biographical film "Selena." Her performance earned her critical acclaim and established her as a formidable actress in Hollywood. Lopez's ability to embody

Selena's spirit and passion resonated with audiences, highlighting her potential to take on diverse and challenging roles.

The Impact and Legacy of a Global Icon

Jennifer Lopez's impact on the entertainment industry extends far beyond her talents as an actress and singer. She has become a cultural icon, breaking barriers and setting new standards for success. Her foray into music in the late 1990s with the release of her debut album "On the 6" marked the beginning of a new era in her career. The album, which included hits like "If You Had My Love" and "Waiting for Tonight," showcased her musical versatility and solidified her status as a pop sensation.

Lopez's music career is characterized by its longevity and evolution. She seamlessly transitioned from pop to Latin music, producing chart-topping hits and collaborating with some of the biggest names in the industry. Her ability to adapt to changing musical landscapes while maintaining her unique style has endeared her to fans across generations. Lopez's success in music is not just measured by her numerous awards and accolades, but by her ability to inspire and connect with a diverse audience.

In addition to her achievements in music and film, Lopez has made significant strides as a businesswoman. She launched her own fashion line, J.Lo by Jennifer Lopez, which became a major success, reflecting her personal style and influence on fashion. Her ventures in the beauty industry, including fragrances and cosmetics, have also been highly successful, further cementing her status as a multifaceted entrepreneur. Lopez's business acumen has allowed her to build an empire, proving that she is not just a performer, but a savvy and innovative business leader.

Lopez's influence extends beyond her professional accomplishments. She has been a powerful advocate for representation and diversity in the entertainment industry. As a Latina woman, she has broken through numerous barriers and challenged stereotypes, paving the way for future generations of artists. Her philanthropic efforts, particularly in education and disaster relief, demonstrate her commitment to giving back to the community and using her platform for positive change.

Throughout her career, Lopez has faced numerous challenges and setbacks, but her resilience and unwavering determination have been a constant. Her personal life, often under the scrutiny of the public eye, has seen its share of highs and lows. Despite this, Lopez has maintained a positive outlook, using her experiences to grow and evolve both personally and professionally. Her ability to navigate the pressures of fame while staying true to herself has earned her respect and admiration worldwide.

Jennifer Lopez's legacy is one of perseverance, talent, and relentless ambition. She has not only achieved extraordinary success in multiple fields but has also become a symbol of empowerment and inspiration. Her journey from the Bronx to global stardom is a testament to the power of dreams and the impact of hard work. As she continues to innovate and push boundaries, Lopez's influence on the entertainment industry and beyond will undoubtedly endure, inspiring countless individuals to pursue their passions and strive for greatness.

Chapter 4: Early Life in the Bronx

Family Background and Childhood

Jennifer Lynn Lopez, born on July 24, 1969, in the Castle Hill neighborhood of the Bronx, New York, is the second of three daughters to Puerto Rican parents Guadalupe Rodríguez and David Lopez. Her mother, a homemaker and kindergarten teacher, and her father, a computer technician, worked tirelessly to provide for their family, instilling in Jennifer and her sisters, Leslie and Lynda, a strong work ethic and the importance of family.

Growing up in a tight-knit household, the Lopez family emphasized the value of togetherness and support. Despite the challenges of living in a working-class neighborhood, the Lopezes maintained a positive and nurturing environment. Jennifer's parents, particularly her mother, recognized her natural inclination toward the arts from an early age. Guadalupe was a major influence in Jennifer's life, often taking her to dance lessons and encouraging her to participate in school plays and local talent shows.

The Lopez family's Puerto Rican heritage played a significant role in shaping Jennifer's identity and aspirations. The vibrant culture of Puerto Rico, with its rich traditions in music, dance, and community, was a constant presence in their home. This cultural backdrop not only influenced Jennifer's artistic interests but also instilled in her a deep sense of pride and connection to her roots. Family gatherings were often filled with music, dancing, and storytelling, fostering an environment where creativity and expression were celebrated.

Jennifer's father, David, was equally influential, providing a different kind of support. As a computer technician working the night shift, David taught Jennifer the importance of perseverance and resilience. His dedication to providing for his family often meant long hours away from home, but his commitment was unwavering. David's work ethic and determination left a lasting impression on Jennifer, reinforcing the belief that hard work and dedication could overcome any obstacle.

The Influence of Puerto Rican Heritage

Jennifer Lopez's Puerto Rican heritage is a fundamental aspect of her identity and has profoundly influenced her career and personal life. Growing up, Jennifer was immersed in the cultural traditions of Puerto Rico, which emphasized the importance of family, community, and a celebratory approach to life. These values are evident in her work, where she often pays homage to her heritage through her music, dance, and public persona.

Puerto Rican music, with its rhythmic beats and passionate lyrics, was a staple in the Lopez household. Genres like salsa, merengue, and reggaeton were frequently played, and Jennifer often danced to these rhythms at family gatherings and community events. This early exposure to Latin music would later influence her own musical style, blending pop with Latin beats to create a unique and captivating sound.

In addition to music, the Lopez family's Puerto Rican heritage influenced their approach to food, holidays, and social gatherings. Traditional Puerto Rican dishes, such as arroz con gandules (rice with pigeon peas), pasteles (savory pastries), and lechón (roast pork), were central to family celebrations. These culinary traditions were not just about food but also about bringing the family together, reinforcing a sense of community and belonging.

The celebration of Puerto Rican holidays and cultural events also played a significant role in Jennifer's upbringing. Festivals like the Puerto Rican Day Parade in New York City highlighted the vibrancy and pride of the Puerto Rican community. Participating in these events fostered a strong cultural identity in Jennifer, making her proud of her heritage and inspiring her to represent her roots on a global stage.

The influence of Puerto Rican heritage extends to Jennifer's strong sense of social responsibility. Puerto

Rican culture places a high value on community support and helping others, which is reflected in Jennifer's philanthropic efforts. She has been actively involved in various charitable initiatives, particularly those aimed at supporting underprivileged communities and disaster relief efforts in Puerto Rico. This commitment to giving back is deeply rooted in the cultural values instilled in her from a young age.

Early Interests and Ambitions

Jennifer Lopez's early life was marked by a myriad of interests and ambitions, many of which foreshadowed her future career in entertainment. From a young age, Jennifer was captivated by the world of performance. Her passion for dance was evident early on, as she started taking lessons in ballet, jazz, and flamenco at just five years old. These lessons were more than just a hobby; they were a foundation for her future endeavors in the entertainment industry.

Jennifer's early dance experiences were formative, teaching her discipline, coordination, and the importance of hard work. She quickly became known for her natural talent and dedication, often spending hours perfecting her routines. Her love for dance extended beyond formal classes, as she frequently participated in school musicals and local talent shows. These performances were Jennifer's first taste of the spotlight, igniting a desire to pursue a career in the performing arts.

In addition to dance, Jennifer developed a keen interest in singing and acting. She would often put on impromptu performances for her family, showcasing her vocal abilities and dramatic flair. Her parents recognized her potential and supported her aspirations, encouraging her to pursue opportunities that would allow her to develop her talents further. This support was crucial in helping Jennifer build the confidence needed to navigate the competitive world of entertainment.

Despite her early passion for the arts, Jennifer's ambitions were not without challenges. Growing up in the Bronx, she faced the difficulties of a working-class neighborhood, where resources and opportunities were limited. However, Jennifer's determination and resilience helped her overcome these obstacles. She balanced her academic responsibilities with her artistic pursuits, demonstrating a remarkable ability to juggle multiple commitments.

Jennifer's high school years were particularly significant in shaping her future. She attended Preston High School, an all-girls Catholic school in the Bronx, where she continued to excel academically and artistically. During this time, Jennifer participated in school productions and dance competitions, further honing her skills and gaining valuable experience. Her talent did not go unnoticed, and she began to gain recognition for her performances.

After graduating from high school, Jennifer briefly attended Baruch College, where she studied business. However, her passion for the arts remained unwavering, and she soon decided to leave college to pursue her dreams full-time. This decision marked a pivotal moment in Jennifer's life, as she took the bold step of dedicating herself entirely to her craft.

Jennifer's early interests and ambitions were driven by a combination of innate talent and a strong support system. Her family's encouragement and her own relentless drive propelled her forward, helping her navigate the challenges and uncertainties of pursuing a career in entertainment. These formative years laid the groundwork for Jennifer's future success, setting the stage for her remarkable journey from the Bronx to global stardom.

Chapter 2: Dancing into the Spotlight

Discovering a Passion for Dance

Jennifer Lopez's journey into the world of dance began at an early age, sparked by an innate passion and a supportive family environment. Growing up in the vibrant and culturally rich neighborhood of the Bronx, Jennifer was exposed to a myriad of musical and dance influences. Her parents, Guadalupe and David Lopez, recognized her enthusiasm for the arts and enrolled her in dance classes when she was just five years old. This early start provided Jennifer with a solid foundation in various dance styles, including ballet, jazz, and flamenco.

Dance quickly became more than just a hobby for Jennifer; it was a form of expression and a source of immense joy. She would often spend hours practicing her routines, demonstrating a level of dedication and discipline that set her apart from her peers. Jennifer's early dance teachers were instrumental in nurturing her talent, providing her with the technical skills and confidence needed to pursue her dreams.

As Jennifer progressed in her dance training, she began to participate in local talent shows and school performances. These opportunities allowed her to showcase her abilities and gain valuable stage experience. Her performances were characterized by a natural grace and charisma that captivated audiences, earning her praise and recognition within her community.

In addition to formal dance classes, Jennifer's exposure to the lively dance culture of the Bronx played a significant role in shaping her style. The neighborhood's rich blend of Latin music, hip-hop, and street dance provided Jennifer with a diverse array of influences. She would often practice her moves at local community centers and participate in dance battles, honing her skills and developing a unique blend of techniques that would later become her signature style.

The Journey to Becoming a Fly Girl on "In Living Color"

Jennifer's passion for dance eventually led her to pursue professional opportunities in the entertainment industry. After graduating from high school, she decided to leave college and focus entirely on her dance career. This decision marked a turning point in Jennifer's life, as she embarked on a journey filled with both challenges and breakthroughs.

Jennifer's big break came when she auditioned for the role of a Fly Girl on the popular television show "In Living Color." Created by Keenen Ivory Wayans, the show was known for its edgy comedy sketches and high-energy dance performances. The Fly Girls, a group of talented female dancers, were a central feature of the show, performing choreographed routines that added a dynamic element to the program.

The audition process for the Fly Girls was highly competitive, attracting dancers from all over the country. Jennifer's determination and unique style set her apart from the other candidates. She impressed the judges with her technical skills, versatility, and stage presence, ultimately earning a spot on the show. Becoming a Fly Girl was a significant achievement for Jennifer, marking her entry into the professional dance world and providing her with a platform to showcase her talents to a national audience.

As a Fly Girl, Jennifer's responsibilities extended beyond just dancing. The role required her to collaborate with the show's choreographers and other dancers, contributing to the creation of innovative routines that captivated viewers. Jennifer's ability to adapt to different dance styles and her commitment to excellence quickly made her a standout performer on the show.

The exposure Jennifer gained from "In Living Color" opened up new opportunities for her in the entertainment industry. Her performances on the show were widely praised, earning her recognition as one of the most talented dancers of her generation. This newfound visibility also led to offers for other projects, including music videos, commercials, and live performances.

Early Struggles and Breakthroughs

Despite her success on "In Living Color," Jennifer's journey to stardom was not without its challenges. The entertainment industry is notoriously competitive, and Jennifer faced numerous obstacles as she sought to establish herself as a versatile performer. Balancing her commitments as a Fly Girl with other professional opportunities required a significant amount of dedication and hard work.

One of the early struggles Jennifer encountered was the constant pressure to prove herself in a male-dominated industry. As a Latina dancer, she often faced stereotypes and biases that questioned her abilities and limited her opportunities. Jennifer's response to these challenges was to work even harder, demonstrating her talent and versatility through her performances.

In addition to external challenges, Jennifer also faced personal struggles. The demanding nature of her work schedule left little time for rest, and the physical toll of constant rehearsals and performances was significant. Despite these difficulties, Jennifer remained focused on her goals, drawing strength from her passion for dance and her unwavering determination.

Jennifer's breakthrough came when she began to transition from dancing to acting. While she continued to pursue dance opportunities, she also started to explore her potential as an actress. Her first major acting role came in the 1995 film "My Family," where she played the character of Maria. This role showcased Jennifer's acting abilities and opened the door to more significant opportunities in Hollywood.

The following year, Jennifer landed a role in the film "Money Train," starring opposite Wesley Snipes and Woody Harrelson. Her performance in the film was well-received, further establishing her as a talented actress. These early acting roles were crucial in helping Jennifer build a diverse portfolio and gain recognition in the entertainment industry.

Jennifer's determination to succeed was evident in her approach to her career. She continuously sought out new opportunities and challenges, never settling for complacency. Her ability to balance multiple aspects of her career, from dancing to acting to eventually singing, showcased her versatility and ambition.

In 1997, Jennifer achieved a major milestone when she was cast as the lead in the biographical film "Selena." Portraying the late Tejano singer Selena Quintanilla-Pérez was a pivotal moment in Jennifer's career, earning her critical acclaim and solidifying her status as a leading actress in Hollywood. The film's success demonstrated Jennifer's ability to take on complex and emotionally charged roles, further expanding her repertoire.

Chapter 3: Breaking into Hollywood

First Roles and Notable Performances

Jennifer Lopez's transition from dancer to actress was marked by her relentless drive to succeed and her willingness to embrace new challenges. After gaining national recognition as a Fly Girl on "In Living Color," Jennifer set her sights on Hollywood, determined to prove herself as a versatile and talented actress. Her journey into the world of acting began with a series of small roles that would eventually lead to significant breakthroughs.

Jennifer's first major acting role came in the 1995 film "My Family" (also known as "Mi Familia"), directed by Gregory Nava. In the film, Jennifer played the young version of Maria, a central character in the story of a Mexican-American family's journey through multiple generations. Although her role was relatively small, Jennifer's performance was notable for its authenticity and emotional depth. Working on "My Family" allowed her to showcase her acting abilities and gain valuable experience in a dramatic role.

Following her work on "My Family," Jennifer continued to pursue acting opportunities, landing a role in the 1995 action-comedy "Money Train." In this film, she starred alongside Wesley Snipes and Woody Harrelson, playing the character of Grace Santiago, a transit cop involved in a heist plot. Jennifer's performance was well-received, and the film provided her with exposure to a broader audience. The role in "Money Train" demonstrated Jennifer's ability to hold her own alongside established actors and highlighted her potential as a leading lady in Hollywood.

Another significant early role for Jennifer was in the 1996 romantic drama "Jack," directed by Francis Ford Coppola. In this film, she played Miss Marquez, a compassionate and supportive schoolteacher who helps the titular character, played by Robin Williams, navigate the challenges of growing up with an unusual medical condition. Working with a director of Coppola's caliber and an actor like Williams was a significant opportunity for Jennifer, allowing her to learn from some of the best in the industry and further refine her craft.

Jennifer's growing body of work during this period included roles in films such as "Blood and Wine" (1996) and "U Turn" (1997). In "Blood and Wine," she starred opposite Jack Nicholson and Michael Caine, playing the role of Gabriela, a young woman caught in a web of deceit and crime. The film was a dark and intense thriller, and Jennifer's performance received critical acclaim for its complexity and nuance. "U Turn," directed by Oliver Stone, saw Jennifer taking on the role of Grace McKenna, a femme fatale in a twisted tale of betrayal and murder. These roles showcased Jennifer's versatility and willingness to tackle challenging and diverse characters.

The Breakthrough Role in "Selena"

Jennifer Lopez's career reached a pivotal moment in 1997 with her portrayal of Selena Quintanilla-Pérez in the biographical film "Selena." Directed by Gregory Nava, who had previously worked with Jennifer on "My Family," the film told the story of the beloved Tejano singer's rise to fame and her tragic death.

Landing the role of Selena was a significant achievement for Jennifer, as it provided her with the opportunity to portray a cultural icon and demonstrate her acting and musical talents.

The casting of Jennifer Lopez as Selena was initially met with some controversy, as fans of the late singer were concerned about whether she could do justice to the role. However, Jennifer's dedication to the project and her deep respect for Selena's legacy quickly won over critics and audiences alike. She immersed herself in the role, studying Selena's mannerisms, voice, and performances to deliver an authentic and heartfelt portrayal.

Jennifer's performance in "Selena" was nothing short of transformative. She captured the essence of Selena's charisma, energy, and warmth, bringing the singer's story to life with sensitivity and grace. The film highlighted Jennifer's ability to convey a wide range of emotions, from the joy of Selena's early successes to the heartbreak of her untimely death. Jennifer's portrayal was widely praised for its authenticity and emotional depth, earning her critical acclaim and several award nominations.

The success of "Selena" was a turning point in Jennifer's career. The film not only introduced her to a global audience but also established her as a formidable talent in Hollywood. Her performance resonated deeply with fans of Selena, as well as with new audiences who were captivated by Jennifer's ability to embody the spirit of the beloved singer. "Selena" remains one of Jennifer's most iconic roles and a testament to her dedication and talent as an actress.

Establishing Herself as a Leading Actress

Following the success of "Selena," Jennifer Lopez's career in Hollywood continued to ascend. She quickly became one of the most sought-after actresses in the industry, known for her versatility and ability to tackle a wide range of roles. Jennifer's determination to establish herself as a leading actress was evident in her choice of projects and her commitment to her craft.

In 1998, Jennifer starred in the crime drama "Out of Sight," directed by Steven Soderbergh. She played the role of Karen Sisco, a federal marshal who becomes entangled with a charming bank robber, played by George Clooney. The film was a critical and commercial success, with Jennifer's performance receiving high praise for its complexity and charisma. Her chemistry with Clooney was particularly noted, and the role further solidified her status as a leading actress capable of carrying a major motion picture.

Jennifer's success in "Out of Sight" was followed by a string of high-profile roles that showcased her range as an actress. In 2000, she starred in the psychological thriller "The Cell," directed by Tarsem Singh. Playing the role of Catherine Deane, a child psychologist who uses experimental technology to enter the minds of her patients, Jennifer delivered a performance that was both haunting and compelling. The film's visually stunning and imaginative approach provided Jennifer with the opportunity to explore a complex and challenging character.

The same year, Jennifer took on a different kind of role in the romantic comedy "The Wedding Planner." Starring opposite Matthew McConaughey, she played Mary Fiore, a successful wedding planner who finds herself falling for one of her clients. The film was a commercial success and demonstrated Jennifer's ability to excel in lighter, comedic roles. Her performance was charming and relatable, further expanding her appeal to a broader audience.

Jennifer's versatility continued to be a defining feature of her career. In 2001, she starred in the drama "Angel Eyes," playing the role of Sharon Pogue, a police officer with a troubled past. The film allowed Jennifer to explore deeper emotional themes and showcase her dramatic acting abilities. Her performance was praised for its intensity and authenticity, further establishing her as a leading actress in Hollywood.

Throughout the early 2000s, Jennifer continued to take on diverse roles, balancing her acting career with her burgeoning music career. She starred in films such as "Maid in Manhattan" (2002), where she played a hotel maid who falls in love with a wealthy politician, and "Shall We Dance?" (2004), where she portrayed a dance instructor who helps a man rediscover his passion for life. These roles highlighted Jennifer's ability to connect with audiences through her relatable and heartfelt performances.

As Jennifer's career progressed, she also began to take on more challenging and unconventional roles. In 2006, she starred in the independent drama "Bordertown," directed by Gregory Nava. The film addressed the issue of femicides in Ciudad Juárez, Mexico, and Jennifer's performance as a journalist investigating the murders was both powerful and poignant. Her commitment to shedding light on important social issues through her work further demonstrated her depth as an actress and her dedication to making a meaningful impact.

In addition to her work in film, Jennifer expanded her influence by becoming involved in television and producing. She served as a judge on the popular reality competition show "American Idol," where she mentored aspiring singers and shared her industry expertise. Jennifer also produced and starred in the hit television series "Shades of Blue," playing the role of Harlee Santos, a corrupt detective navigating the challenges of her personal and professional life. The series received positive reviews and showcased Jennifer's ability to excel in complex and multifaceted roles.

Chapter 4: Versatility on Screen

Memorable Roles in Romantic Comedies

Jennifer Lopez's versatility as an actress is perhaps most evident in her performances in romantic comedies, a genre where she has consistently shone. Her ability to bring charm, relatability, and depth to her characters has made her a favorite in this genre, appealing to a broad audience.

One of her most iconic roles in romantic comedies is that of Mary Fiore in "The Wedding Planner" (2001). In this film, Jennifer plays a successful wedding planner who meticulously organizes other people's weddings but has yet to find love herself. Her character's journey from professional detachment to personal vulnerability is handled with a deft touch, blending humor and heart. The chemistry between Jennifer and her co-star, Matthew McConaughey, was palpable, making their on-screen romance believable and engaging. Jennifer's performance in "The Wedding Planner" solidified her status as a leading lady in romantic comedies, demonstrating her ability to carry a film on her own.

Following "The Wedding Planner," Jennifer starred in "Maid in Manhattan" (2002), another successful romantic comedy that showcased her ability to portray characters with warmth and authenticity. In this film, she plays Marisa Ventura, a hotel maid who is mistaken for a wealthy socialite by a high-profile politician, played by Ralph Fiennes. The film explores themes of class and identity, and Jennifer's portrayal of Marisa's struggles and aspirations resonated with audiences. Her performance was praised for its relatability and charm, further establishing her as a beloved figure in the genre.

Jennifer continued to build on her success with "Shall We Dance?" (2004), where she starred opposite Richard Gere. In this film, she played Paulina, a dance instructor who helps Gere's character rediscover his passion for life through ballroom dancing. The film was a departure from traditional romantic comedies, focusing more on personal growth and transformation. Jennifer's performance was both graceful and inspiring, highlighting her ability to bring depth to her characters even in a light-hearted setting.

In "Monster-in-Law" (2005), Jennifer took on the role of Charlie, a woman who finds herself at odds with her overbearing future mother-in-law, played by Jane Fonda. The film's comedic premise allowed Jennifer to showcase her comedic timing and ability to handle physical comedy. Her performance was lauded for its energy and humor, and her dynamic with Fonda added an extra layer of entertainment to the film.

Jennifer's ability to seamlessly transition between various tones within romantic comedies was further exemplified in "The Back-up Plan" (2010). In this film, she played Zoe, a single woman who decides to become a mother through artificial insemination, only to meet the man of her dreams shortly after. The film's exploration of unconventional paths to love and family provided Jennifer with the opportunity to portray a modern, independent woman navigating complex emotions. Her performance was praised for its warmth and relatability, reinforcing her status as a versatile actress capable of handling diverse romantic scenarios.

Tackling Dramatic Roles

While Jennifer Lopez has found significant success in romantic comedies, her dramatic roles have also played a crucial part in showcasing her versatility and depth as an actress. Jennifer has proven that she can tackle complex and emotionally demanding characters with nuance and intensity.

One of Jennifer's most acclaimed dramatic roles came in the 1998 film "Out of Sight," directed by Steven Soderbergh. In this crime drama, she played Karen Sisco, a U.S. Marshal who becomes entangled with a charming bank robber, portrayed by George Clooney. The role required Jennifer to balance toughness with vulnerability, and she delivered a performance that was both compelling and memorable. Her chemistry with Clooney was a highlight of the film, and their dynamic added depth to the storyline. Jennifer's portrayal of Karen Sisco showcased her ability to handle intricate character arcs and complex emotional landscapes.

In 2002, Jennifer took on the challenging role of Slim Hiller in the thriller "Enough." The film follows Slim, a woman who escapes an abusive marriage and fights back against her violent husband. Jennifer's portrayal of a woman reclaiming her strength and autonomy was powerful and resonated with audiences. The role required her to perform intense physical scenes and convey a wide range of emotions, from fear and desperation to determination and empowerment. Jennifer's performance in "Enough" was praised for its authenticity and strength, highlighting her capability to handle demanding dramatic roles.

Another significant dramatic role for Jennifer came in the 2006 film "Bordertown," directed by Gregory Nava. In this film, she played Lauren Adrian, a journalist investigating the murders of women in Ciudad Juárez, Mexico. The film addressed serious social issues, and Jennifer's portrayal of a determined and courageous journalist brought attention to the plight of the victims. Her performance was both passionate and poignant, reflecting her commitment to bringing important stories to the forefront. "Bordertown" allowed Jennifer to delve into a character with a strong sense of justice and purpose, showcasing her ability to take on roles with social and political relevance.

In 2015, Jennifer starred in the independent drama "Lila & Eve," alongside Viola Davis. The film told the story of two mothers who take justice into their own hands after their children are murdered. Jennifer's portrayal of Eve, a grieving mother driven by anger and sorrow, was raw and intense. Her performance captured the deep emotional pain and desperation of a parent who has lost a child, and her chemistry with Davis added a powerful dynamic to the film. "Lila & Eve" demonstrated Jennifer's ability to tackle dark and emotionally challenging roles with sensitivity and depth.

Jennifer's dramatic range was further showcased in the 2019 film "Hustlers," where she played Ramona Vega, a savvy and charismatic stripper who leads a group of women in a scheme to con wealthy men. The role was a departure from her previous work, allowing her to explore a character with moral ambiguity and complex motivations. Jennifer's performance was widely praised, earning her several award nominations, including a Golden Globe nod. Her portrayal of Ramona was both captivating and layered, highlighting her ability to bring complexity and nuance to her characters.

Working with Hollywood A-Listers

Throughout her career, Jennifer Lopez has had the opportunity to work with some of Hollywood's most renowned actors and directors, further solidifying her status as a versatile and respected actress. Collaborating with A-listers has not only enhanced her performances but also provided her with valuable experiences that have contributed to her growth as an artist.

In "Out of Sight," Jennifer's on-screen partnership with George Clooney was a significant highlight. Their chemistry was electric, and their performances complemented each other perfectly, making the film a standout in both their careers. Working with Clooney, an established actor with a strong presence, allowed Jennifer to elevate her performance and demonstrate her ability to hold her own alongside a major star.

Jennifer's collaboration with Richard Gere in "Shall We Dance?" was another notable pairing. Gere, a veteran actor known for his charisma and charm, brought a seasoned presence to the film, while

Jennifer's fresh and inspiring portrayal of a dance instructor added a dynamic contrast. Their on-screen relationship was both touching and believable, contributing to the film's success.

In "Monster-in-Law," Jennifer had the opportunity to work with Jane Fonda, an icon of the film industry. Fonda's portrayal of the overbearing and eccentric mother-in-law was a perfect foil to Jennifer's character, creating a comedic and entertaining dynamic. Working with Fonda provided Jennifer with the chance to learn from a legendary actress and further hone her comedic timing.

Jennifer's role in "The Cell" allowed her to collaborate with Vincent D'Onofrio, a talented actor known for his intense and transformative performances. Their scenes together were gripping and psychologically complex, adding depth to the film's narrative. Jennifer's ability to match D'Onofrio's intensity and bring her own unique energy to the role demonstrated her versatility and range as an actress.

In "Hustlers," Jennifer worked with a talented ensemble cast, including Constance Wu, Keke Palmer, and Lili Reinhart. The film's success was largely due to the strong performances and chemistry among the cast members. Jennifer's role as the leader of the group required her to bring a commanding and charismatic presence to the screen, and her interactions with her co-stars were both engaging and dynamic. The collaborative environment of "Hustlers" showcased Jennifer's ability to work effectively in a team and contribute to a compelling ensemble performance.

Chapter 5: The Birth of a Pop Star

The Release of "On the 6" and Initial Success

Jennifer Lopez's foray into the music industry marked a new chapter in her already multifaceted career. In 1999, she released her debut studio album, "On the 6," a title inspired by her roots in the Bronx and the subway line she used to take to Manhattan for auditions and performances. The album's release signaled Jennifer's ambition to expand her artistic horizons beyond acting and dancing.

"On the 6" was a significant departure from Jennifer's previous work as a dancer and actress. The album blended pop, Latin, and R&B influences, reflecting Jennifer's diverse musical tastes and cultural background. The lead single, "If You Had My Love," was a chart-topping hit that showcased Jennifer's sultry vocals and confident stage presence. The song's music video, which featured Jennifer in various futuristic settings, became a cultural phenomenon and solidified her status as a rising star in the music industry.

Following the success of "If You Had My Love," Jennifer released several more singles from "On the 6," including "Waiting for Tonight" and "Let's Get Loud." These songs further showcased Jennifer's versatility as an artist, with "Waiting for Tonight" becoming a staple of dance floors worldwide and "Let's Get Loud" celebrating her Latin heritage with its infectious rhythms and empowering lyrics.

Collaborations with Music Industry Giants

As Jennifer Lopez's music career gained momentum, she had the opportunity to collaborate with some of the music industry's most influential artists and producers. These collaborations not only expanded Jennifer's musical repertoire but also cemented her place in the pop music landscape.

One of Jennifer's notable collaborations came in 2000 with rapper Ja Rule on the hit single "I'm Real." The song, which featured a remix with Ja Rule's signature rap verses, became a chart-topper and showcased Jennifer's ability to seamlessly blend pop and hip-hop elements. The success of "I'm Real" further solidified Jennifer's crossover appeal and introduced her to a broader audience.

In 2001, Jennifer collaborated with rapper and producer Sean "Diddy" Combs on the single "Love Don't Cost a Thing." The song, which was featured on Jennifer's second studio album, "J.Lo," became a commercial success and emphasized her ability to deliver catchy hooks and infectious melodies. The collaboration with Diddy highlighted Jennifer's knack for working with top-tier talent and solidified her reputation as a pop powerhouse.

Jennifer continued to collaborate with music industry giants throughout her career, including collaborations with Pitbull, LL Cool J, and Pitbull. These collaborations further expanded Jennifer's musical palette and allowed her to explore different genres and styles.

Defining the J.Lo Sound

One of Jennifer Lopez's contributions to the music industry has been her ability to craft a distinct sound that blends pop sensibilities with Latin rhythms and urban influences. From her early hits to her later releases, Jennifer has maintained a consistent musical identity that resonates with fans around the world.

The "J.Lo sound" is characterized by its infectious beats, memorable hooks, and Jennifer's dynamic vocals. Her music often features elements of dance-pop, R&B, and Latin music, reflecting her diverse musical influences and cultural background. Songs like "Let's Get Loud," "Jenny from the Block," and

"On the Floor" have become anthems that celebrate Jennifer's Bronx roots while appealing to a global audience.

Jennifer's ability to infuse her music with personal experiences and emotions has also been a key aspect of the "J.Lo sound." Her lyrics often explore themes of empowerment, love, and resilience, resonating with listeners who connect with her authenticity and vulnerability. Jennifer's music has evolved over the years, reflecting her growth as an artist and her willingness to experiment with new sounds and collaborations.

In addition to her solo career, Jennifer has also contributed to the music industry through her work as a featured artist and guest vocalist. Her collaborations with other artists have allowed her to explore different genres and expand her artistic horizons. Jennifer's versatility as a performer has enabled her to seamlessly transition between acting, dancing, and music, solidifying her status as a triple threat in the entertainment industry.

Chapter 6: Chart-Topping Success

Hit Singles and Albums

Jennifer Lopez's career in music has been marked by a series of chart-topping singles and successful albums that have solidified her status as a global pop icon. From her early days with "On the 6" to her more recent releases, Jennifer's ability to consistently deliver catchy hooks and infectious melodies has endeared her to fans around the world.

Following the success of her debut album, "On the 6," Jennifer continued to release hit singles that dominated the charts. In 2001, she released her second studio album, simply titled "J.Lo." The album featured the smash hit single "Love Don't Cost a Thing," which became an anthem for empowerment and independence. The song's catchy chorus and upbeat production resonated with audiences, earning Jennifer widespread acclaim and further solidifying her place in the music industry.

Jennifer's third studio album, "This Is Me... Then," released in 2002, showcased a more personal and introspective side of the artist. The album's lead single, "Jenny from the Block," became a cultural phenomenon, celebrating Jennifer's Bronx roots and addressing the challenges of fame and public scrutiny. The song's autobiographical lyrics and catchy melody struck a chord with listeners, who embraced its message of staying true to oneself despite success.

In 2005, Jennifer released "Rebirth," her fourth studio album, which featured the hit singles "Get Right" and "Hold You Down." The album marked a stylistic shift for Jennifer, incorporating elements of hip-hop and dance music into her sound. "Get Right," in particular, became a club favorite and showcased

Jennifer's versatility as an artist who could effortlessly blend genres and styles.

Jennifer's success continued with the release of her sixth studio album, "Love?" in 2011. The album's lead single, "On the Floor," featuring Pitbull, became one of Jennifer's biggest hits to date. The song topped charts worldwide and became a global anthem for dance and celebration. Its infectious beat and memorable chorus propelled Jennifer back into the spotlight, reaffirming her status as a powerhouse in pop music.

World Tours and Live Performances

In addition to her studio albums and hit singles, Jennifer Lopez's career has been defined by her electrifying live performances and world tours. Known for her dynamic stage presence and high-energy routines, Jennifer has captivated audiences across the globe with her larger-than-life shows.

Jennifer embarked on her first world tour, the "Let's Get Loud Tour," in 2001, following the success of her debut album. The tour showcased Jennifer's versatility as a performer, featuring a mix of pop hits, dance numbers, and heartfelt ballads. With sold-out shows in major cities around the world, the "Let's Get Loud Tour" solidified Jennifer's reputation as a must-see live performer and established her as a global superstar.

Throughout her career, Jennifer has continued to thrill fans with memorable live performances at prestigious events and venues. From the Super Bowl halftime show to awards ceremonies and music festivals, Jennifer's stage presence and charisma have consistently earned rave reviews from critics and fans alike. Her ability to command the stage and connect with audiences through her music and choreography has made her a standout in the world of live entertainment.

Awards and Recognitions

Jennifer Lopez's chart-topping success and influential impact on popular culture have been recognized with numerous awards and accolades throughout her career. From Grammy nominations to prestigious honors, Jennifer's talent and contributions to music have garnered acclaim from industry peers and fans worldwide.

Jennifer received her first Grammy Award nomination in 2000 for Best Dance Recording for "Waiting for Tonight." Although she did not win that year, the nomination highlighted her ability to deliver memorable and impactful music that resonated with audiences.

In 2003, Jennifer received the American Music Award for Favorite Pop/Rock Female Artist, solidifying her status as a beloved figure in the music industry. The award recognized Jennifer's popularity and influence among fans of pop music and underscored her ability to connect with audiences through her music and performances.

Throughout her career, Jennifer has continued to receive accolades for her achievements in music, film, and television. She has been honored with multiple MTV Video Music Awards, Billboard Music Awards, and People's Choice Awards, among others. Jennifer's versatility as an entertainer and her ability to excel in multiple disciplines have earned her a place among the entertainment industry's elite.

Chapter 7: The Business Mogul

Launching Fashion Lines and Fragrances

Jennifer Lopez's entrepreneurial spirit extends beyond her music and acting career into the realm of fashion and beauty. Known for her impeccable style and trendsetting looks, Jennifer has successfully launched several fashion lines and fragrance collections that reflect her distinctive sense of fashion and appeal to fans worldwide.

In 2001, Jennifer launched her first fashion line, J.Lo by Jennifer Lopez, which featured a range of casual wear, accessories, and fragrances. The collection was inspired by Jennifer's personal style and included denim jeans, tops, and accessories that captured her glamorous yet approachable aesthetic. The success of J.Lo by Jennifer Lopez demonstrated Jennifer's ability to translate her fashion sense into a commercially viable brand and solidified her status as a fashion icon.

Building on the success of her initial fashion venture, Jennifer expanded her brand with the launch of Sweetface Fashion Company in 2003. The luxury fashion line featured high-end clothing and accessories designed to appeal to a more upscale market. Jennifer's involvement in the design process and her commitment to quality and craftsmanship helped distinguish Sweetface as a sought-after fashion brand.

In addition to her clothing lines, Jennifer has also found success in the fragrance industry with the launch of several signature fragrances. Her debut fragrance, "Glow by J.Lo," launched in 2002, became an instant bestseller and established Jennifer as a major player in the fragrance market. The success of "Glow by J.Lo" was followed by a series of additional fragrances, including "Still Jennifer Lopez," "Live Luxe," and "Glowing Goddess," each capturing different facets of Jennifer's personality and style.

Jennifer's ability to leverage her celebrity status and personal brand to create successful fashion and fragrance lines has earned her respect in the business world. Her keen sense of style, combined with her business acumen, has allowed her to navigate the competitive fashion industry and establish herself as a formidable entrepreneur.

Building a Production Empire

Beyond her achievements in music and fashion, Jennifer Lopez has also made significant strides in the entertainment industry as a producer and businesswoman. Jennifer's production company, Nuyorican Productions, was founded in 2001 and has since become a powerhouse in film, television, and digital content.

Nuyorican Productions was responsible for producing Jennifer's breakthrough film, "El

Cantante" (2006), in which she starred alongside Marc Anthony. The biographical drama told the story of salsa legend Hector Lavoe and showcased Jennifer's versatility as both an actress and producer. The film received critical acclaim for its authenticity and emotional depth, solidifying Jennifer's reputation as a producer with a keen eye for compelling storytelling.

In addition to producing films, Nuyorican Productions has been involved in creating successful television shows and digital content. Jennifer served as an executive producer for the television series "The Fosters" (2013-2018), which received praise for its portrayal of diverse family dynamics and social issues. The show's success underscored Jennifer's commitment to producing meaningful and impactful content that resonates with audiences.

Nuyorican Productions has also ventured into digital media with the launch of original content for online platforms. Jennifer's production company has developed web series, documentaries, and digital shorts that showcase diverse voices and explore contemporary themes. By embracing digital platforms, Nuyorican Productions has demonstrated its ability to adapt to changing media landscapes and reach new audiences worldwide.

Entrepreneurial Endeavors and Investments

In addition to her fashion lines and production company, Jennifer Lopez has diversified her portfolio through various entrepreneurial endeavors and investments. Jennifer's business acumen and strategic investments have allowed her to build a successful and diverse portfolio that extends beyond entertainment and fashion.

Jennifer has been actively involved in real estate investments, acquiring properties in desirable locations across the United States. Her keen eye for design and architecture has led to successful renovations and developments that have increased the value of her real estate holdings. Jennifer's investments in real estate reflect her long-term financial strategy and commitment to building wealth through strategic acquisitions.

Jennifer has also ventured into the hospitality industry with the launch of her restaurant chain, Madre's. The upscale dining establishments feature a blend of Latin and Mediterranean cuisine, reflecting Jennifer's cultural heritage and culinary preferences. The success of Madre's restaurants has allowed Jennifer to expand her footprint in the hospitality sector and establish herself as a restaurateur with a commitment to quality and innovation.

Chapter 8: Personal Triumphs and Tribulations

High-Profile Relationships and Marriages

Jennifer Lopez's personal life has often been the subject of intense media scrutiny, particularly her high-profile relationships and marriages. Throughout her career, Jennifer has been romantically linked to several prominent figures in the entertainment industry, each relationship leaving a lasting impact on her personal journey.

One of Jennifer's most notable relationships was with actor and producer Sean "Diddy" Combs, whom she dated from 1999 to 2001. Their romance captivated the public's attention, as both were rising stars in their respective fields. Despite their busy schedules and the pressures of fame, Jennifer and Diddy shared a passionate and dynamic relationship that was closely followed by fans and the media.

Following her relationship with Diddy, Jennifer married choreographer Cris Judd in 2001. Their marriage, however, was short-lived, and they divorced less than a year later. Despite the challenges of their brief union, Jennifer and Cris remained amicable and supportive of each other's careers.

In 2002, Jennifer's highly publicized engagement to actor Ben Affleck garnered widespread media attention. The couple, often referred to as "Bennifer" by the media, seemed poised for a fairy-tale romance, with plans for a lavish wedding and a future together. However, their relationship faced intense scrutiny from the media and public, which ultimately took its toll on their engagement. Jennifer and Ben called off their wedding in 2004, marking the end of one of Hollywood's most scrutinized relationships.

In 2004, Jennifer married singer Marc Anthony, with whom she had previously collaborated musically. Their marriage produced twins, a son named

Maximilian David and a daughter named Emme Maribel, born in 2008. Jennifer and Marc's union was celebrated by fans and marked a new chapter in Jennifer's personal life, as she embraced motherhood and family.

Motherhood and Family Life

Motherhood has been a transformative experience for Jennifer Lopez, who has embraced her role as a mother with love and dedication. Jennifer's twins, Maximilian and Emme, were born in 2008 and have been a source of joy and inspiration in her life.

Jennifer has been open about the challenges of balancing her career with motherhood, describing it as a rewarding yet demanding experience. She has emphasized the importance of family and creating a stable and loving environment for her children, despite the pressures of her high-profile career.

In addition to her twins with Marc Anthony, Jennifer has embraced a blended family dynamic. Marc Anthony has children from previous relationships, and Jennifer has welcomed them into her life with open arms. The family's bond is evident in their public appearances and social media posts, showcasing their love and support for each other.

As a mother, Jennifer has been actively involved in her children's lives, attending school events, sports games, and family vacations. She has prioritized creating lasting memories with her children and instilling values of hard work, perseverance, and kindness.

Overcoming Personal Challenges

Throughout her life and career, Jennifer Lopez has faced personal challenges and setbacks that have tested her resilience and strength. One of the most difficult periods in Jennifer's life was her highly publicized divorce from Marc Anthony in 2014. The end of their marriage was a deeply emotional time for Jennifer, who navigated the pain of separation while balancing her responsibilities as a mother and entertainer.

Despite the challenges of divorce, Jennifer remained focused on her children and her career, finding solace in music, acting, and the support of loved ones. She channeled her emotions into her work, using music as a form of expression and healing.

In addition to personal relationships, Jennifer has faced professional challenges that have shaped her career and personal growth. Throughout her journey, she has encountered criticism, setbacks, and moments of self-doubt. However, Jennifer's resilience and determination have allowed her to overcome obstacles and emerge stronger than ever.

Jennifer Lopez's ability to navigate personal triumphs and tribulations with grace and resilience has made her an inspiration to fans around the world. Her openness about her experiences has helped break down barriers and stigma surrounding relationships, motherhood, and personal struggles. Jennifer continues to evolve as an artist, entrepreneur, and mother, embracing life's challenges and triumphs with courage and authenticity.

Chapter 9: Cultural Impact

Representation and Advocacy

Jennifer Lopez's influence extends far beyond her achievements in music, film, and business. Throughout her career, Jennifer has been a vocal advocate for representation and diversity in entertainment, using her platform to amplify marginalized voices and promote inclusivity.

As a Latina woman of Puerto Rican descent, Jennifer has been a trailblazer in Hollywood, challenging stereotypes and paving the way for greater representation of Latinx talent on screen. Early in her career, Jennifer faced skepticism and barriers as she pursued roles that reflected her heritage and identity. However, she persisted in advocating for roles that showcased the diversity and richness of Latinx culture.

Jennifer's breakthrough role in the biographical film "Selena" (1997), where she portrayed the iconic Tejano singer Selena Quintanilla-Pérez, was a pivotal moment in her career and for Latinx representation in mainstream media. The film celebrated Selena's cultural heritage and musical legacy while highlighting Jennifer's ability to embody complex and authentic characters. Jennifer's portrayal earned her critical acclaim and solidified her status as a talented actress capable of transcending cultural boundaries.

Throughout her career, Jennifer has continued to champion representation both in front of and behind the camera. She has been involved in producing projects that feature diverse casts and narratives, ensuring that Latinx stories are told with authenticity and respect. Jennifer's production company, Nuyorican Productions, has been instrumental in developing projects that celebrate cultural diversity and showcase the talents of underrepresented communities.

In addition to her work in entertainment, Jennifer has been a passionate advocate for social justice and equality. She has used her platform to raise awareness about issues affecting marginalized communities, including immigration reform, civil rights, and gender equality. Jennifer's advocacy efforts have included participating in marches, speaking engagements, and charitable initiatives aimed at creating positive change.

Inspiring the Next Generation

Jennifer Lopez's impact on popular culture extends beyond her artistic achievements to her role as a mentor and inspiration to aspiring artists and entrepreneurs. Throughout her career, Jennifer has encouraged young people to pursue their dreams and embrace their cultural heritage with pride.

Jennifer's journey from the Bronx to global stardom has inspired countless individuals who see themselves reflected in her story of perseverance and determination. She has been vocal about the importance of hard work, resilience, and believing in oneself, regardless of obstacles or setbacks.

Jennifer has mentored aspiring performers through programs like "Q'Viva! The Chosen," a talent competition show that sought to discover and showcase Latinx talent from around the world. The show highlighted Jennifer's commitment to nurturing the next generation of artists and providing opportunities for diverse voices to be heard.

In addition to her work in entertainment, Jennifer has been actively involved in educational initiatives and philanthropic efforts aimed at empowering young people. She has supported programs that provide access to arts education, mentorship, and career development opportunities for underserved youth, believing in the transformative power of education and mentorship.

Contributions to Latinx Visibility

Jennifer Lopez's contributions to Latinx visibility in entertainment and popular culture have been significant and enduring. As one of the most prominent Latina entertainers in the world, Jennifer has used her platform to challenge stereotypes and elevate the representation of Latinx talent across various mediums.

Jennifer's success in music, film, and television has shattered barriers and opened doors for other Latinx artists seeking recognition and opportunities in Hollywood. Her ability to seamlessly navigate between genres and roles has showcased the diversity and depth of talent within the Latinx community, challenging industry norms and expanding perceptions of what it means to be a Latina artist.

Jennifer's influence on Latinx visibility extends beyond her individual achievements to her advocacy for greater representation and opportunities in the entertainment industry. She has been outspoken about the need for more diverse storytelling and the importance of authentic representation in media.

Conclusion

Throughout Jennifer Lopez's illustrious career, spanning music, film, fashion, and entrepreneurship, she has left an indelible mark on the entertainment industry and popular culture. From her humble beginnings in the Bronx to becoming a global superstar, Jennifer's journey is a testament to perseverance, passion, and the power of believing in oneself.

Reflecting on her career, Jennifer Lopez acknowledges the challenges and triumphs that have shaped her path. She has shared intimate moments of self-discovery and growth, from navigating the highs and lows of fame to finding balance between her professional ambitions and personal life. Jennifer's authenticity and vulnerability have resonated with fans worldwide, inspiring them to embrace their own journeys with courage and resilience.

Jennifer Lopez's journey is marked by valuable lessons learned along the way. She emphasizes the importance of hard work, dedication, and perseverance in achieving one's dreams. Jennifer encourages aspiring artists to stay true to themselves, embrace their unique talents, and never be afraid to take risks. She underscores the significance of resilience in the face of adversity and the power of self-belief in overcoming obstacles.

Jennifer Lopez's legacy extends far beyond her accomplishments in music, film, and business. She has redefined standards of beauty and success, challenging stereotypes and paving the way for greater diversity and representation in entertainment. Jennifer's impact on Latinx visibility and cultural representation continues to resonate, inspiring future generations to embrace their heritage and pursue their passions fearlessly.

As a multifaceted artist and entrepreneur, Jennifer Lopez has demonstrated an unwavering commitment to innovation and creativity. Her contributions to fashion and fragrance have redefined industry norms, while her entrepreneurial ventures have diversified her influence beyond entertainment. Jennifer's production company, Nuyorican Productions, has fostered meaningful storytelling and amplified marginalized voices, underscoring her dedication to inclusivity and social impact.

Jennifer Lopez's journey is a testament to the transformative power of artistry, resilience, and cultural pride. Her legacy as a trailblazer in entertainment and business continues to inspire and empower individuals around the world. Jennifer's ability to transcend boundaries and break barriers reflects her enduring influence and her commitment to leaving a lasting impact on future generations. As she continues to evolve as an artist, mentor, and advocate, Jennifer Lopez remains a beacon of strength, creativity, and authenticity in an ever-changing world.

Printed in Dunstable, United Kingdom